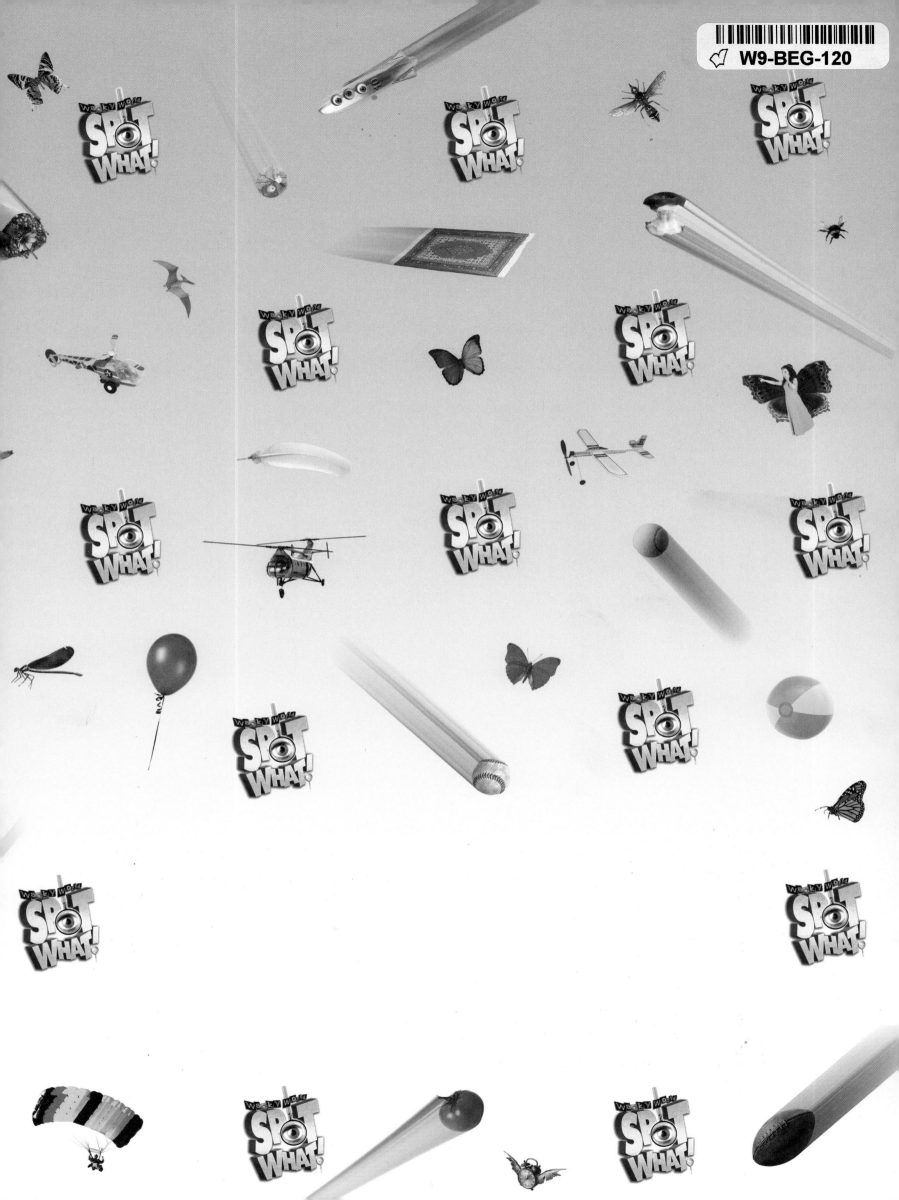

WACKY WORLD

SPOT WHAT!

Sandy Creek

Magnifying glass

Cat

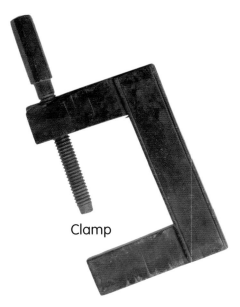

Clamp

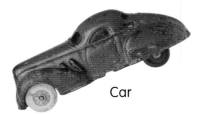

Car

Creators: Nick Bryant and Rowan Summers
Cover design: Peter Tovey
Prepress: Graphic Print Group

Sandy Creek
387 Park Avenue South
New York, NY 10016

ISBN: 978 1 4351 3728 8

Printed and bound in Heshan, China
Manufactured August 2011

Lot 1 3 5 7 9 10 8 6 4 2

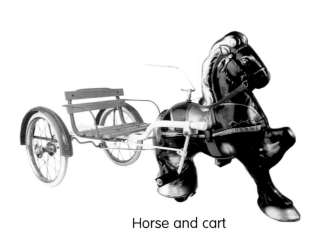

Horse and cart

Cello

Contents

Pine cone

Clarinet

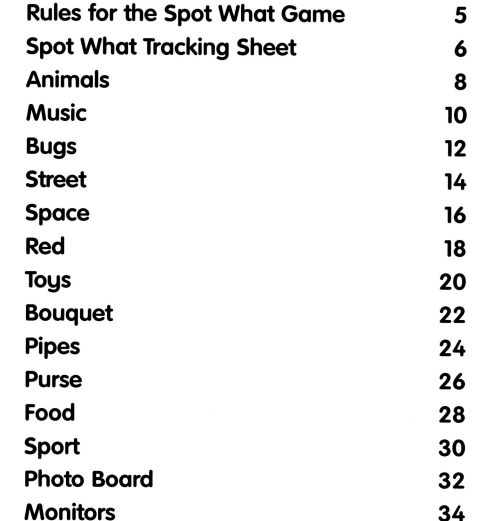

Lizard

Candelabra

Chequered flag

Trumpet

Wacky World Spot What

Welcome to **Spot What 3D**!

Are you prepared to take the **Spot What** challenge?
Can you find all the items cleverly hidden amongst the pages?
Test your spotting skills and see how many you can find!

Each page has a list of items that have been concealed within the images on the page. Work your way through the lists and see just how good a spotter you are!

We've also included some extra challenges at the end of the book. Can you find these extra-hard-to-spot items?

You can take on the challenge by yourself or you can battle against another person to discover who the ultimate spotting champion is! We have provided the rules for the **Spot What** spotting game.

Don't forget, some of the pages in this book are presented using amazing three-dimensional technology. Use the terrific 3D glasses that come with this book to give you a whole new dimension on the **Spot What** challenge!

Have fun, and good luck spotting!

Rules for the Spot What Game

1. Flip a coin to see who goes first. The winner of the coin toss is 'the caller' and the other player is 'the spotter'.

2. The caller chooses a page from the book and picks an item for the spotter to find, saying, for example, 'Can you spot a rocket ship?'

3. The spotter must then try to find the item.

4. If the spotter can't find it, the caller gets 5 points and shows the spotter where it is and has another turn.

5. If the spotter can find the item, then he or she gets 5 points and now it's his or her turn to be the caller.

6. The first to reach 30 points wins but you could also set your own limit or simply play best out of three!

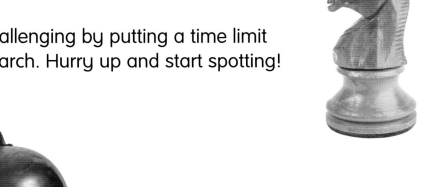

You can make the game more challenging by putting a time limit of one to three minutes on each search. Hurry up and start spotting!

Spot What Tracking Sheet

Use this sheet to track which **Spot What** activities you have completed.
Once you have spotted all the items listed, place a ✔ in the box beside each activity.

Remember, though, only true **Spot What** superstars will be able to fill in the whole sheet!

• Activity Pages

Animals		Music		Bugs	
Street		Space		Red	
Toys		Bouquet		Pipes	
Purse		Food		Sport	
Photo Board		Monitors		Underwater	
Tools		Bedroom		Games	
Blue		Spectacles		Nature	
Case		House		Stamps	

• The **Spot What** Challenge

Animals		Music		Bugs	
Street		Space		Red	
Toys		Bouquet		Pipes	
Purse		Food		Sport	
Photo Board		Monitors		Underwater	
Tools		Bedroom		Games	
Blue		Spectacles		Nature	
Case		House		Stamps	

Can you spot two elephants,
Three giraffes and a bat,
A lion, a tiger, a leopard,
An owl and a pussycat?

Can you find four eagles,
Three dogs, a hippo, a moose,
A sheep, a mouse and a rabbit,
A golden egg and a goose?

Find a saxophone, a gramophone,
A xylophone, a flute,
Four guitars, three tiny stars,
A golden harp and a lute.

Music makes the world go round,
There's a ukulele and a clarinet,
Seven trumpets can be found,
A golden bell and maraca set.

11

Can you spot a cotton reel,
A nib, a tag and a plug,
A yacht, a die, a bolt, a door key
And a bright red ladybug?

Can you find three house flies,
A needle and a caterpillar,
Two centipedes, two spiders,
A hook, a nail and a gorilla?

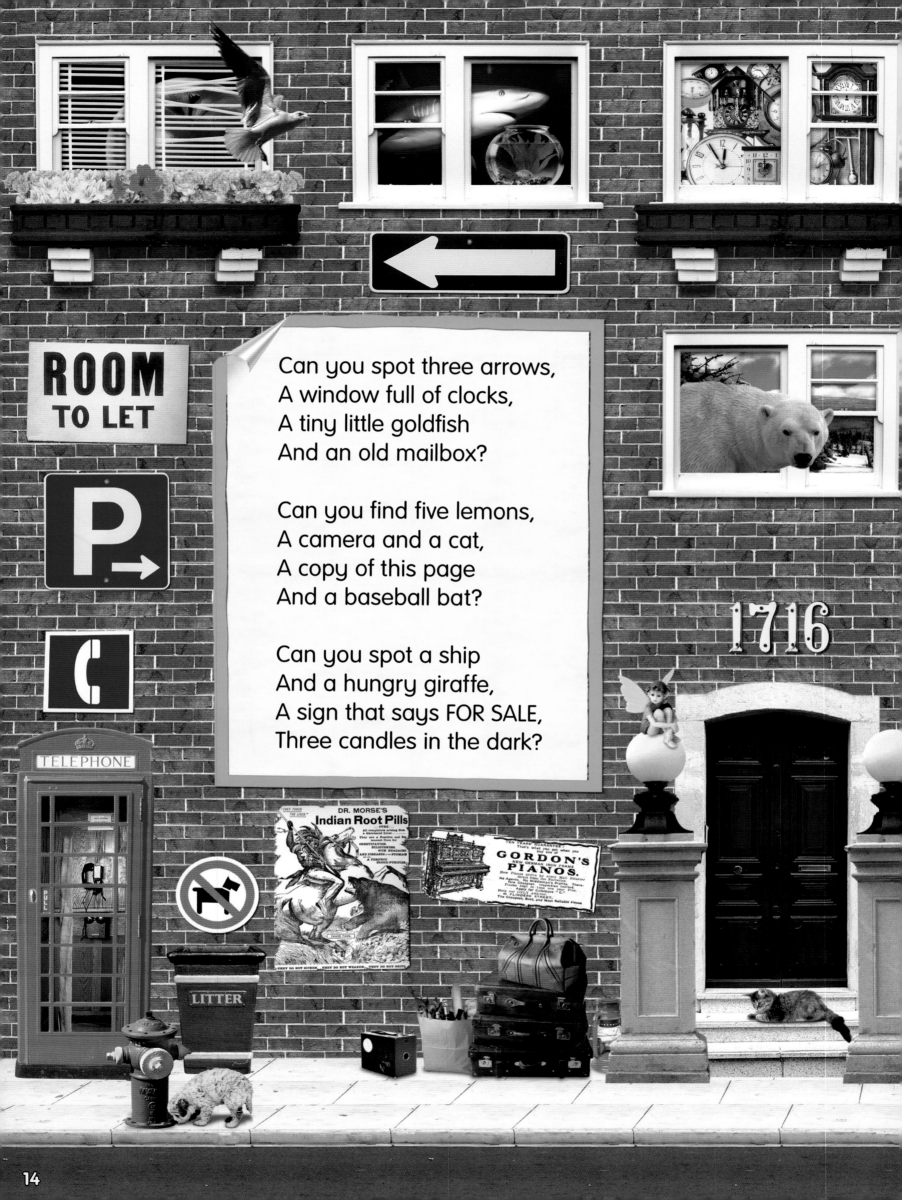

Can you spot three arrows,
A window full of clocks,
A tiny little goldfish
And an old mailbox?

Can you find five lemons,
A camera and a cat,
A copy of this page
And a baseball bat?

Can you spot a ship
And a hungry giraffe,
A sign that says FOR SALE,
Three candles in the dark?

ROOM
TO LET

TELEPHONE

1716

DR. MORSE'S
Indian Root Pills

GORDON'S
PIANOS.

LITTER

Can you spot a magnet, a CD and TV,
A sailing ship, a house and a chimpanzee,
A barrel, a bottle and four starfish,
Five astronauts and a satellite dish?
Find a golf ball and a horse with wings,
A nut, a bolt and planetary rings.

Can you spot
A bus and a train,
A monkey wrench
And a jet plane?

Six strawberries,
Find them all,
A pair of lips
And a ping-pong ball.

Can you find
A big toolbox,
A Christmas hat and
Two Christmas socks?

Can you spot a wooden plane,
A piano and a house,
A tractor, trike and windmill,
A little wind-up mouse?

Can you find three horses,
A carrot in a truck,
A tambourine, a sewing machine
And a fluffy yellow duck?

Can you spot a ball of wool,
A stapler and a fan,
A wagon wheel, a fishing reel,
An egg and frying pan?

Find a candelabra,
A knife, a fork and a pie,
A banjo and a compass,
An umbrella and bow tie.

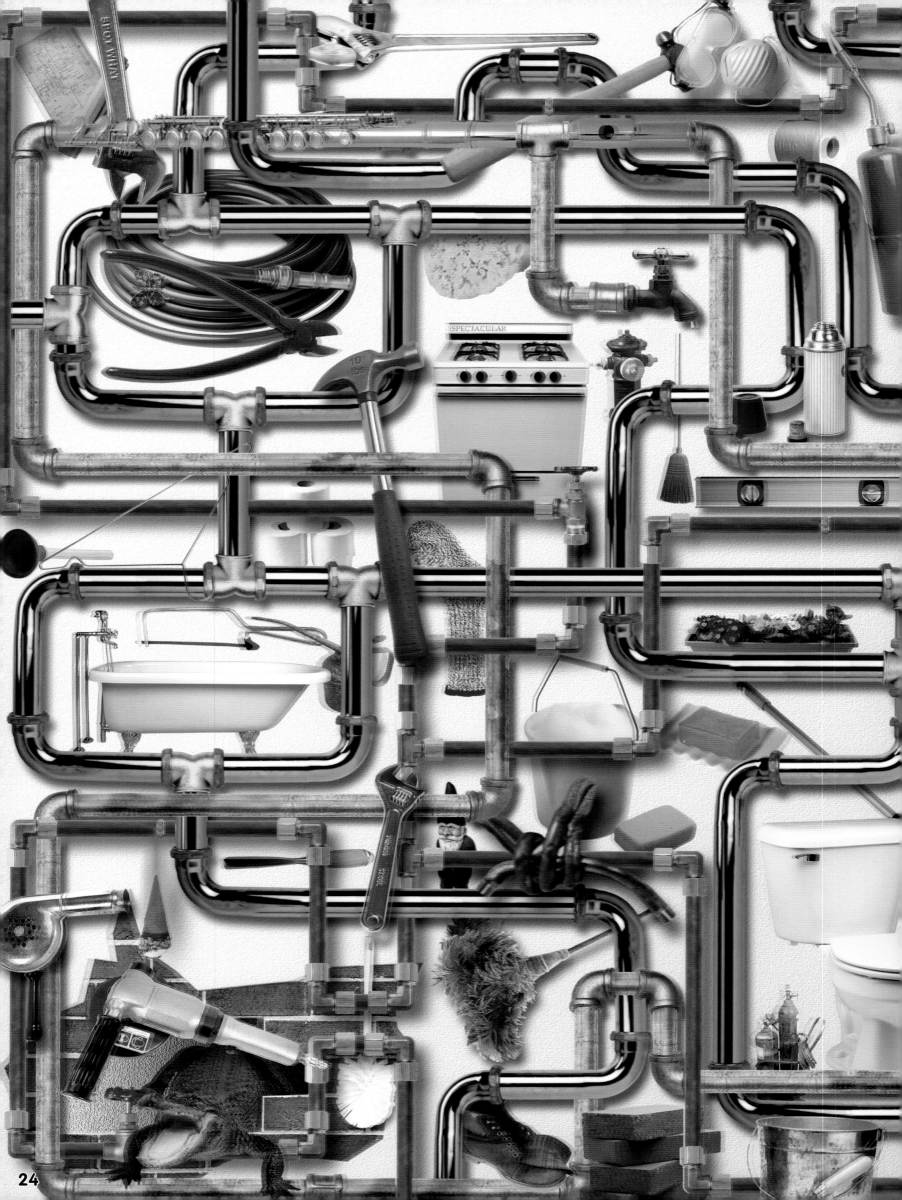

Can you find
 a pair of socks,
A stove, a bath,
 a flowerbox,
A pump, a nail,
 a refrigerator,
A broom, a snail
 and an alligator?
Find five hammers,
 three buckets, a boot,
Two plungers,
 two sponges,
A ladder, a flute.

Can you spot a set of keys,
And a red lipstick,
Seven coins, a pack of gum,
And a little candlestick?

Can you spot three brushes,
And a sticky first-aid strip,
Golden wings, five shiny rings,
And a tiny pair of lips?

To you with love

Can you spot an apple core,
A bunch of grapes, a soft-drink can,
Corn on the cob and two hot dogs,
A carrot and a gingerbread man?

Can you find a pizza pie,
Three different types of cheese,
An avocado, half a tomato
And four little honeybees?

SPOT WHAT

ADMIT ONE
SPORTING
SPECTACULAR
0596033
0596033

Can you spot a basketball,
A tennis ball, two bats,
A skipping rope, a bowling ball,
A fisherman's hat?

Find a pair of ice skates,
Two whistles and a dart,
A stopwatch, a chequered flag,
A saddle, a horse and cart.

☺ The Bank of Smiles

To: Mother Hubbard
Address: The Shoe
         Nursery Land

01/01/2000

The more you invest in life, the more you get back from it.

A smile costs nothing, but can mean so much.

Account balance:

1/12/1999   Deposit   12 laughs
             Deposit   17 hugs
             Deposit   34 smiles

             Withdrawal   9 tears

Lower Upper Overshot Highway

Station Street

stern Street

HAPPY BIRTHDAY

y most beloved,

How happy I was to   received your last letter.
rvellous to read all a   e
nds very exciting.
en raining here almo
garden, but it does mu
've heard that others are going to follow your
   Mr. Butcher, Mr. Baker and t local Ca
all set off to sea in a tub no less.   on't kn
worthiness of such items but I'm re that i
I'm sure you will be joining r as so
            you very much and want
                        nearts.

All more to

WIT
MY L

Note

Shopping List:
4 x Bones for the dog.
2 x tins of dog food
1 x bottle of milk
1 Packet of dog biscuits
1 Bottle of dog shampoo
Flea Powder
hair brush

Can you spot a spider,
A medal and a boat,
A telephone, a turtle
And a little love note?

Can you find a bicycle,
A violin and feather,
A map, three green tacks
And five kittens all together?

9th

Can you spot a goldfish,
An apple and cartoon,
A skier, wolf and tomahawk,
A spider and baboon?

Find a bear, a skunk, a poodle,
And a slide trombone,
A donkey and a lobster,
A watch and microphone.

Can you spot a jellyfish,
A seahorse and two skulls,
A turtle and a lighthouse,
One pearl and two seagulls?

Find five leaping dolphins,
A crab, a pair of oars,
An octopus, a treasure chest,
A coin, a kettle, a door.

SS SPECTACULAR

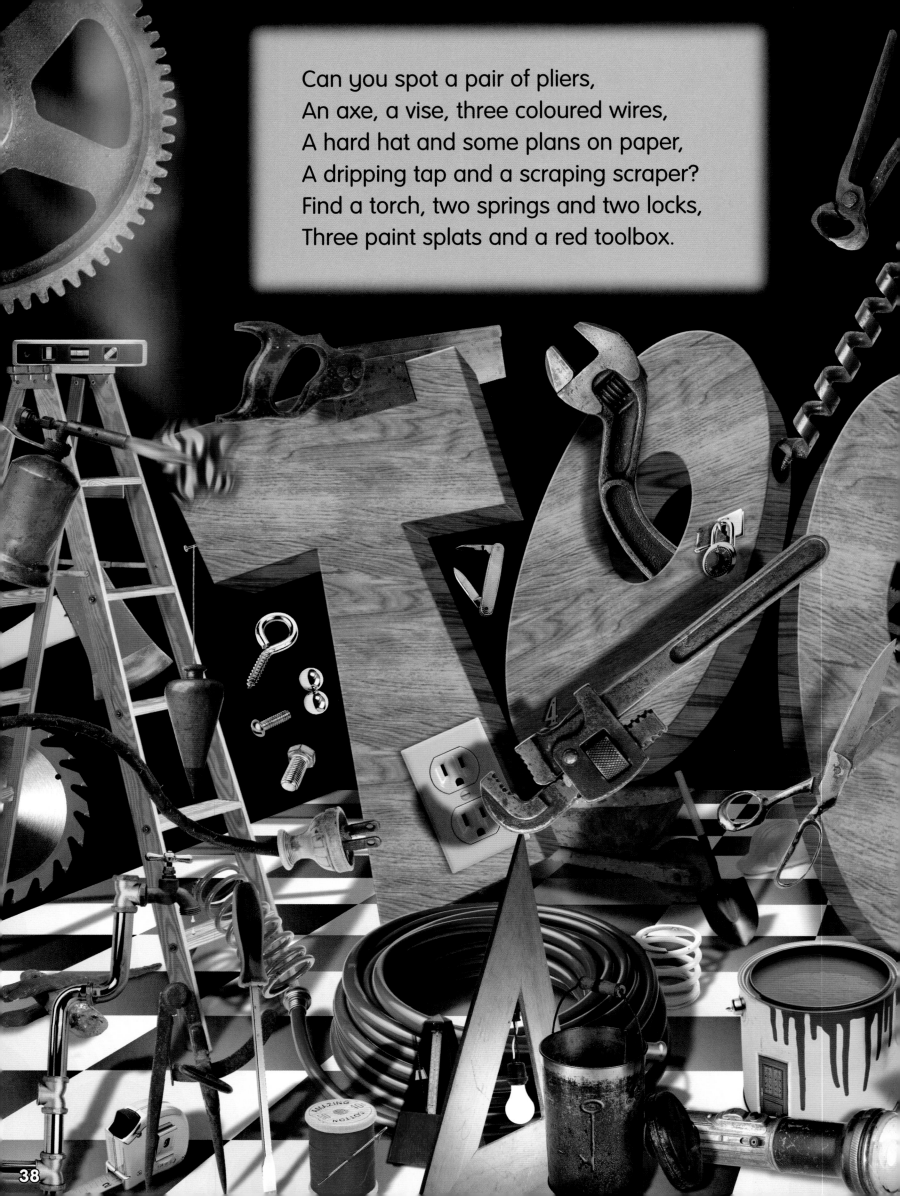

Can you spot a pair of pliers,
An axe, a vise, three coloured wires,
A hard hat and some plans on paper,
A dripping tap and a scraping scraper?
Find a torch, two springs and two locks,
Three paint splats and a red toolbox.

Can you spot a pumpkin head,
Three balls and a dragon,
Two lizards and a wizard
And a little red wagon?

Can you find a pair of gloves,
Two orange boots and a frog,
A car, a train, a cowboy,
Three mice, two cats, four dogs?

POEM
OF THE DAY

Can you spot three dominoes,
Two giraffes and tick-tack-toe,
Three red dice, another blue,
A pawn, a knight and a joker too?
Find eight jacks, a queen, a king,
Two darts, a clown and a yoyo string.

42

Can you spot a bird and a pen,
A telephone and ten past ten,
A truck, a puppet, two buckets, a tie,
A rabbit, a boot and a butterfly?
Find a jukebox, a feather, a star,
A whistle, a flipper, a drum and guitar.

Can you spot a birthday cake,
A telephone, a ring,
A rattle and a thimble,
A ladybug, a wing?

Can you find a lobster,
An eyeball and a key,
A skier and an ice cube,
A log, a nest, a tree?

47

AMAZING FALLS →

Can you spot a kangaroo,
Five daisies and a snake,
A soccer ball, a pineapple,
A hose, a spade, a rake?

Can you find a squirrel,
A shuttlecock, a gnome,
Three fairies, a canary,
And five pine cones?

Collected things from many lands
Are stored within a case.
Can you spot two clowns, a coin,
A sad and happy face,
Two ducks, two dogs, two horses,
Two ways of telling time,
Three locks, five eggs, a pumpkin head
And a red stop sign?

51

Can you spot
A pair of scissors,
A wagon wheel
And a shiny mirror,

A pyramid
And a clock,
A dinosaur,
A hose, a sock?

There's a happy ghost,
An old-fashioned hat,
A pair of boots
And a dancing cat.

Can you spot five paperclips
And a Chinese boat,
A rhinoceros, an elephant
And a mountain goat?

Find the stamp from Musicland
And a human brain,
A camel and a croissant,
A jet and two biplanes.

The Spot What Challenge

See if you can spot these things in the pages listed:

Hourglass

Mermaid

Blue door

Can you find the words 'SPOT WHAT',
A mermaid and a four,
A ladybug, a light bulb
And a little blue door?

Light bulb

Apple

Gnome

Ice-cream cone

Fairy

Can you find the words 'SPOT WHAT',
The number ten, a gnome,
A butterfly, an hourglass
And an ice-cream cone?

Ladybug

Butterfly

Can you find the words 'SPOT WHAT',
A fairy and a three,
A matchstick and an apple
And a honey bee?

Matchstick

Bee

57

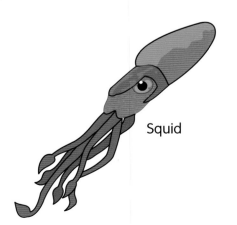

Dog

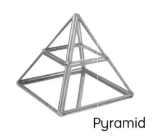

Pyramid

The following items are much harder to find, so get ready for the challenge!

Animals
(pages 8/9)

A frog
3 wise monkeys
3 lizards
2 feathers
Early bird gets worm
A spider and a fly
A snail

Music
(pages 10/11)

A banjo
An accordian
A pair of castanets
A bee
A tin whistle
Bongo drums

Ice-cream cone

Bugs
(pages 12/13)

Butterfly A
Butterfly B
Butterfly C
A knight in armour
A pig
4 clown faces

Street
(pages 14/15)

3 shoes
6 ducks
A lantern
A scary smile
A bonsai garden
A mirror on the wall

Squid

Gnome

Message
in a bottle

Old radio

Space

(pages 16/17)

All 12 zodiac symbols
A parking meter
A picnic
A space shuttle
4 telescopes
Venus and Mars
A kazoo

Red

(pages 18/19)

A tractor
Bolt cutters
A hardhat
A feather
A clamp
2 boxing gloves

Mermaid

Toys

(pages 20/21)

2 dinosaurs
An egg beater
A hammer and a wrench
A lion
A purse
The cow that jumped over the moon

Bouquet

(pages 22/23)

A ship's wheel
An elephant
A gramophone
A fluffy bunny
A pair of ballet shoes
A guitar
A swan

Metronome

Wagon wheel

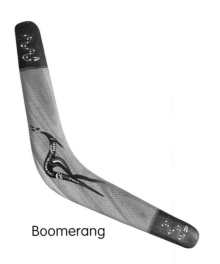

Boomerang

Cowboy

Pipes

(pages 24/25)

A teapot
5 toilet rolls
An egg
A coat hanger
A fire hydrant
A toilet brush
A set of plans

Purse

(pages 26/27)

5 diamonds
A frog
A cat
A pair of scissors
An umbrella
A ticket to Wonderland
A pen

Dogfish

Food

(pages 28/29)

3 balloons
3 chilli peppers
Some teeth
A Christmas tree
6 individual peanuts
6 blue candles
6 strawberries

Sport

(pages 30/31)

A yoyo
A hockey puck
5 soccer balls
A boomerang
2 catcher's mitts
2 shuttlecocks
2 pair of binoculars

Wagon

Tuning
fork

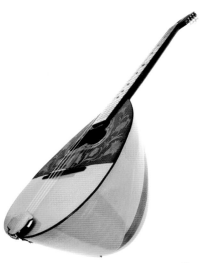

Lute

Butterfly

Photo Board

(pages 32/33)

9 brass tacks
The words 'HAPPY BIRTHDAY'
Noughts and crosses
A piano player
A butterfly
A helicopter

Monitors

(pages 34/35)

7 escaped butterflies
A potted plant
A rock band
A door handle
A jack
2 cameras
'CHANNEL 17'

Underwater

(pages 36/37)

A catfish and a dogfish
4 starfish
4 scuba divers
A seal
2 anchors
A message in a bottle
7 seashells

Tools

(pages 38/39)

5 keys
A needle
3 cogs
3 measuring tools
3 different saws
A microscope
A metronome

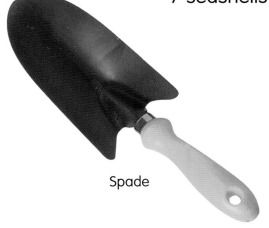

Spade

The Thinker

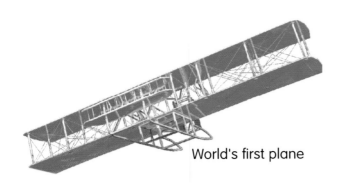

World's first plane

Soft-drink can

Bedroom
(pages 40/41)

4 dinosaurs
23 yellow stars
An elephant
6 musical instruments
A fairy
A green plane
7 bears

Games
(pages 42/43)

A fishbowl
A dog
4 flies
A thimble
Solitaire game
A pig
14 marbles

Wooden plane

Blue
(pages 44/45)

A typewriter
A seahorse
12 musical notes
5 fish
4 boats
4 balls
A rocking chair

Spectacles
(pages 46/47)

A diamond
A rhinoceros
A light bulb
A fishbowl
9 marbles
A mirror
A jack

Toy soldier

Egg with legs

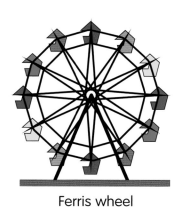

Ferris wheel

Ukulele

Nature

(pages 48/49)

A spider
An owl
A hungry bee
A nest
2 lizards
7 snails
A hummingbird

Case

(pages 50/51)

2 owls
A musical note
A lizard
2 knights in armour
The Thinker
A Viking ship

House

(pages 52/53)

Zodiac symbol

7 keys
A fire engine
A skull
A radio
3 chess pieces
The numbers 1, 2 and 4

Stamps

(pages 54/55)

2 leopards
2 stamps from Nowhere
3 kings
A tiger
A lion
A stamp worth 4 peanuts

Tomahawk

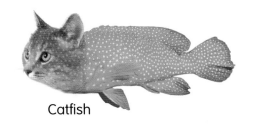

Catfish

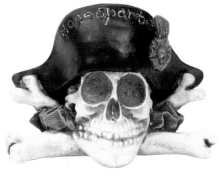

Skull

Ball

Acknowledgements

We would like to thank the following people:

Sam Bryant
Suzanne Buckley
Sante Cigany
Claire Tennant
Dingeling Bros Circus
Samantha Boardman
Kendra Bishop
Derek Debenham
Rod and Mary Bryant
Louise Coulthard
Silvana Paolini
Stephen Ungar
Stephen Bishop
Kendra Bishop
Tracey Ahern

Sam Grimmer
Peter Wakeman
Peter Tovey Studios
Kate Bryant
Paul Scott
Tommy Z
Toby Bishop
Kristie Maxwell
Kelly-Anne Thompson
Miles Summers
Ruth Coleman
Heather Hammonds
Christopher Timms
Gillian Banham
Alison McDonald

Albert Meli from Continuous Recall
Qi Crystals Fossils Minerals, Melbourne, Vic
Little Ashlie, Michael, Nicole and James for lending their toys
Everyone at Hinkler Books

Furniture for 'Bedroom' created by Christopher Peregrine Timms
www. christophertimms.com.au
Thanks to Tsutomu Higo for the use of geometric models for 'Numbers'
www.asahi-net.or.jp/~nj2t-hg/

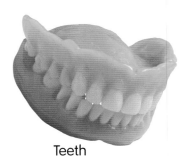

Teeth

Nib

Rocking horse

Diamond